THE

CHRISTIAN MINISTRY.

A SERMON

PREACHED BEFORE THE NEW YORK PREACHERS' MEETING,
MONDAY, FEBRUARY 8, 1876,

BY

BISHOP E. S. JANES, D.D., LL.D.

REPORTED BY WILLIAM ANDERSON.

NEW YORK:
NELSON & PHILLIPS.
CINCINNATI:
HITCHCOCK & WALDEN.
1876.

THE

CHRISTIAN MINISTRY.

A SERMON

PREACHED BEFORE THE NEW YORK PREACHERS' MEETING,
MONDAY, FEBRUARY 8, 1876,

BY

BISHOP E. S. JANES, D.D., LL.D.

REPORTED BY WILLIAM ANDERSON.

NEW YORK:
NELSON & PHILLIPS.
CINCINNATI:
HITCHCOCK & WALDEN.
1876.

THE

CHRISTIAN MINISTRY.

If any man speak, let him speak as the oracles of God; if any man minister, let him do it as of the ability which God giveth; that God in all things may be glorified through Jesus Christ: to whom be praise and dominion for ever and ever. Amen.—1 PETER iv, 11.

I LATELY sat by the death-bed of our beloved and cherished Dr. Wakeley; and on perceiving that the final hour was near, I said to him, "Brother Wakeley, what shall I say from you to your brethren in the ministry?" He opened his eyes, and looked at me with an expression of intense interest, and said promptly, and with all the emphasis which his strength would permit—being only able to utter a few words at a time, because of difficulty of breathing: "Say to them what Peter says: 'If any man speak, let him speak as the oracles of God; if any man minister, let him do it as of the ability which God giveth; that God in all things may be glorified through Jesus Christ.'" And subsequently he added the expression: "To whom be praise and dominion for ever and ever. Amen." It has seemed to me that I shall have no other opportunity of speaking to so many who were actually associated with him in his ministry, and who knew him so intimately, as are here this morning; and that is one consideration which has influenced me in the selection of this passage as the subject of my remarks this hour. O that I could preach from it as I believe he would preach from it, could he this morning come from his state of beatitude and address us on these topics!

The *subjects* presented in the passage are so apparent and so distinct that you will have all perceived them before I state them: The rule of religious speaking —"as the oracles of God;" the measure of religious ministration—"as of the ability which God giveth;" the only motive to influence us in thus speaking and ministering—"that God in all things may be glorified through Jesus Christ." These directions are applicable to all who are speaking and working for Jesus; they are particularly applicable to the minister and the Christian pastor, and in this limited application I shall consider them at this time.

If any minister speak, let him speak as the Bible, as the Holy Scriptures, as the oracles of God, "speak." Let all his conversation be such as becometh the Gospel; but especially in his public teachings, in his religious discourses, in preaching, let him speak according to this rule. We might infer the duty of thus doing from his office. As ministers, we are not speaking for ourselves; we are not advocating any cause of our own; we are not seeking to promote any plan or purpose that we have formed. We are representative men—in the language of the Discipline, "messengers, watchmen, and stewards of the Lord;" and the apostle terms us embassadors for Christ—representatives of the Saviour. The Bible contains our written instructions, and we cannot transcend them. We must not come short of them. We are not authorized to modify them. We must conform to them.

We learn this, also, from the example of the apostles: "We preach not ourselves, but Christ Jesus the Lord; and ourselves your servants for Jesus' sake." "We preach . . . Christ the power of God and the wisdom of God." "I am pure from the blood of all men. For I have not shunned to declare unto you all the counsel of God." "Having therefore obtained help of God, I continue unto this day, witnessing both to small and great, saying none other things than those which the prophets and Moses did say should come: that Christ should suffer, and that he should be the first that should rise from the dead, and should show light unto the people, and to the Gentiles." Our instructions are exceedingly explicit on this subject: "Preach the word;" "Go ye into all the world, and preach my Gospel to every creature;" "To the law and to the testimony: if they speak not according to this word, it is because there is no light in them." The law of fitness and of propriety is as rigid and absolute on this subject as either of those teachings to which we have referred. Our Discipline, also, is very direct and clear on this subject. In our ordination service these two questions are propounded to each candidate, and he is expected to give an affirmative answer or the service to cease: "Are you persuaded that the Holy Scriptures contain sufficiently all doctrine required of necessity for eternal salvation through faith in Jesus Christ? And are you determined out of the said Scriptures to instruct the people committed to your charge, and to teach nothing as required of necessity to eternal salvation, but that which you shall be persuaded may be concluded and proved by the Scriptures?" To qualify us for this, this other question is submitted: "Will you be diligent in prayers, and in reading of the Holy Scriptures, and in such studies as help to the knowledge of the same, laying aside the study of the world and the flesh?"

During the ordination service in the case of deacons, the candidate, laying his hand upon the open Bible, the administrator addresses to him these words: "Take thou authority to read the Holy Scriptures in the Church of God, and to preach the same." In the ordination of elders, in the same solemn form, the administrator says to the person being ordained: "Take thou authority as an elder in the Church, to preach the word of God, and to administer the holy sacraments in the congregation." There is no other license given to ministers of our Church in any part of our Discipline, or in these ordination services. We are shut up to this one rule: "Speak as the oracles of God."

In this country, and at this time, there are two particularly strong temptations to depart from this rule. The one is, to preach science. The references of Holy Scripture to science are very frequent. Scientific knowledge is useful. Ministers have spent years of labor and study to acquire this knowledge; and at the present day there are some claiming for themselves to be pre-eminently scientists, who are seeking to exalt human science above divine inspiration. Under all these provocations it is no wonder that sometimes ministers are not only tempted to depart from the rule we have referred to, but yield to that temptation to some extent. We think, however, that an examination of the Scriptures on this subject will enable us to see the propriety of resisting this temptation. The Holy Scriptures do not teach science; they use it. There is no chapter or paragraph or verse in the Bible employed for the purpose of teaching science. That is not within the design of Holy Scripture. But the Holy Scripture uses science as an instrument by which to elucidate, illustrate, and represent spiritual and divine things, enabling us the more fully to perceive and apprehend them; but in every case science serves, not directs; it is an assistant, and not the chief agent.

For illustration, the psalmist, in presenting to us the divine majesty, the wisdom and power of the Infinite, exclaims: "The heavens declare the glory of God; and the firmament showeth his handywork. Day unto day uttereth speech, and night unto night showeth knowledge. There is no speech nor language, where their voice is not heard. Their line is gone out through all the earth, and their words to the end of the world." And again, in representing human character, and the scale of being in which we are found, he says: "When I consider thy heavens, the work of thy fingers, the moon and the stars, which thou hast ordained; what is man, that thou art mindful of him? and the son of man, that thou visitest him? Thou hast made him a little lower than the angels, and hast crowned him with glory and honor. Thou madest him to have dominion over the works of thy hands." Dr. Young employs this science in like manner:—

"Behold this midnight glory! worlds on worlds!
Amazing pomp! redouble this amaze;
Ten thousand add, and twice ten thousand more!
One soul outweighs them all.
And why? Because it is immortal.

In neither of these cases are we taught the science of astronomy; but in both instances astronomy is made to illustrate the objects which the speaker had in view, the representation of the characters of God and of man, and of the relations of one and the interests of the other. Our Saviour uses the science of chemistry in representing the work of truth and grace in the human soul, and also the operations of the Gospel upon the human family. "The kingdom of heaven is like unto leaven, which a woman took and hid in three measures of meal, till the whole was leavened." Here is no discussion of the subject of chemistry; here is no presentation of that science; here is no talk of the elective affinities and of the action of one substance upon another. Our Lord takes the simple fact, known to the common people as well as to the learned, and by that figure illustrates most beautifully and forcefully the sublime truth that his grace can sanctify human nature and his Gospel recover our world. When I was a young man, before I began to preach, I heard a man of high reputation and of eminent position in the Church preach from that text. He spent a whole hour in describing to us the properties of flour and the properties of leaven, and the action of one upon the other—all the chemical affinities involved in the case—and after he had spent an hour in that scientific lecture he took ten or fifteen minutes, in a hurried and very unsatisfactory manner, to describe to us the influence of grace upon the human heart. I said to myself then, and I am of the same opinion now, He had better have been a school-master than a minister.

In illustrating one of the greatest mysteries and

one of the sublimest doctrines of Christianity, the apostle borrows figures drawn from the science of agriculture. In speaking of the resurrection of the human body he says: "It is sown in dishonor, it is raised in glory: it is sown in weakness, it is raised in power: it is sown a natural body, it is raised a spiritual body." Here we have the seeding and the harvest—a representation of how the harvest gathered exceeds in glory the seed sown—an illustration which, perhaps, is the most fitting and the clearest which could be found in all the realm of nature to illustrate that great mystery. But we need not add more. We think these illustrations are sufficient to show the difference between teaching science and using it, and that in the Holy Scriptures the use of it, and not the teaching of it, is found; and that if we speak "as the oracles of God," we shall do likewise.

The minister is to use his science just as the general uses his. When he sees the foe advance upon him in line of battle he does not go out in the presence of the enemy and deliver a lecture on military tactics, or military engineering, or the science of gunnery. That would be ridiculous. Neither does he load his cannon with text-books, diagrams, or mathematical propositions. These would never batter down the ramparts of the enemy, nor arrest the oncoming column. But he uses his science in planting his batteries, in sighting his guns, in determining the quantity and character of the ammunition he is to employ to reach a certain point and effect a certain object. His science is seen in its results; his science is seen in his victories, and nowhere else. That should be the manner in which we should employ our science and learning ; in planting the batteries of truth ; in so directing the enginery of the Gospel as to reach the human conscience, as to break down the strongholds of sin ; in so throwing the arrows of the Almighty that they shall be sharp in the hearts of the King's enemies, and thereby overthrowing the powers of darkness and the wickedness of men, and subjugating men's hearts and lives to the precepts and the love of our Lord Jesus Christ. Our science should be seen in our revivals and in the conversions under our ministrations. And for this purpose the minister is advantaged by all science and by all knowledge. It will be an advantage to him if he can subordinate the whole universe to this object ; if he can draw his illustrations, figures of speech, and aids in enlightening the minds and hearts of his people from the whole arcana of nature.

Another temptation against which we should guard is, the preaching of politics. We have such a grand country, such glorious institutions, such rich enfranchisements, that no wonder the patriotism of an intelligent man should be intense, and that under his fervor he should become enthusiastic in his admiration of the institutions and immunities of the country in which he lives, and that he should be extremely desirous of promoting, by every opportunity and influence he may possess, those measures, plans, views, and sentiments which he thinks should prevail and obtain in order to the highest welfare of the nation. Consequently, it is no marvel that he should sometimes feel it to be a duty, even in the pulpit, to speak on these subjects. We can hardly find it in our hearts to blame a man who, under such inspirations, should sometimes deviate from the rule prescribed in our text; yet, perhaps, it may be well for us to look at this question calmly for a few moments. The Bible does not prescribe any form of civil government. It has left the form of government to the people. Consequently, the Bible does not advocate any political measures, nor does it advocate any political sentiments, or even institutions, merely as political ones, aside from the general one of government.

The Bible, however, does most distinctly set forth the doctrine of governmental morals, and the word of God does most fully instruct us in the duties of citizenship. Hear the word of the Lord on these points: "Righteousness exalteth a nation; but sin is a reproach to any people;" a statement that comprehends the whole question of national morals. "He that ruleth over men must be just, ruling in the fear of God;" and "rulers are not a terror to good works, but to the evil." Now inasmuch as the Bible—the oracles of God—which are our rule in preaching, thus set before us these great moral aspects of the subject, they become legitimate topics for our ministration. Therein is to be found the justification for the preaching of the last half century on the moral aspects of slavery. So long as ministers in the pulpit confined themselves to that aspect of the question, they created public sentiment, and public sympathy, and public conscience, and they were promoting the great interest which they sought to effect; but, in my judgment, when they left the moral aspects for the political side of the question, they weakened their power on this topic.

Here, too, is our authority for preaching on the

subject of temperance. The Bible instructs us that no drunkard shall inherit the kingdom of heaven. Drunkenness is a crime of such enormity that it excludes from the kingdom of grace and glory. Verily, it is one of the sins to be set before the people. "Woe unto him that giveth his neighbor drink, that puttest thy bottle to him, and makest him drunken." I believe that that involves not only direct, but indirect agency; and the individual who manufactures intoxicating drinks, and who traffics in intoxicating drinks, and the man who sustains a social custom that puts the bottle to his neighbor, and who by his example encourages drunkenness, is under this "woe;" and it is the duty of every minister, in every pulpit, and under every circumstance, to lay this responsibility upon the people. There is no other power that can banish this terrible vice from our land, or deliver our world from this enormous wickedness.

Here, too, is our authority for preaching on the sanctity of the Sabbath. That is an institution of God. It is in the same decalogue with the commandments, "Thou shalt not steal," and, "Thou shalt not kill." God, by his authority, expressly requires that we keep that day holy. The sanctity of that day is essential to the public morals; it is essential to the physical welfare of society, and to the permanency of our civil and religious institutions. If we speak according to the "oracles of God," we cannot fail to set before the people the claims of this day by the authority and requirement of God, the supreme Governor of heaven and of earth.

God has also, in the Bible, established the marriage relation; and he has given to us the laws by which that relation is to be governed; and he has declared that though they be man and woman, when united in holy wedlock the twain become one flesh, and that they cannot be separated by any legislative device, or by any authority of the State, for any other cause than that of adultery on the part of one or the other, or of both. And in order that we may maintain the sacredness and the sweetness of our homes, and protect childhood and youth, we must cultivate the public sentiment on this subject until the laws of the State are in harmony with the laws of God.

The Bible requires of us that we train up our children in the way in which they should go—in the nurture and admonition of the Lord. It is not a subject to be neglected by the Church or the State. The proper training of children is not only one of the highest duties of society, but, as we have seen, one upon which God has spoken. And if we "train up a child in the way he should go," we have the assurance that "when he is old he will not depart from it." God also says in his book, "For the soul to be without knowledge it is not good." It becomes us to see that this training and education are given under such circumstances as to secure the moral and religious life of these children, because, according to the passage we have quoted, their future manhood will be in striking accordance with their childhood—with its circumstances, and the influences under which it is passed, and the direction which is then given to it. This is a question that ought to be considered by us with great carefulness. We are to mold, as far as possible, public sentiment and the national action into harmony with the teachings and precepts of God's most holy word on this subject.

We now call your attention to the other point we named—that of citizenship. The apostle says, that we must be subject to the powers that be, "whether it be to the king, as supreme; or unto governors, as unto them that are sent by him for the punishment of evil doers, and for the praise of them that do well." Recognize constituted authority, and obey it. That is the first claim of citizenship. A citizen is to pay his taxes. When Jesus came to Capernaum on a certain occasion, they that received tribute money said to Peter, "Doth not your Master pay tribute?" Peter answered, "Yes." And when he was come into the house, Jesus prevented his submitting the question to him by asking him, "Of whom do the kings of the earth take custom or tribute? of their own children, or of strangers?" Peter answered, "Of strangers." Jesus said, "Then are the children free. Notwithstanding, lest we should offend them, go thou to the sea, and cast a hook, and take up the fish that first cometh up; and when thou hast opened his mouth, thou shalt find a piece of money: that take, and give unto them for me and thee." Jesus wrought a miracle to pay taxes, and he required of his disciples that they should meet this claim of the Government; and I here affirm that that man who cheats the Government is just as wicked as the man that cheats his neighbor. That individual who refuses to pay duty, or to pay taxes, and robs his Government, is just as much a robber as he who robs his fellow-men. We cannot dodge this question of sustaining the Government by paying duties and our taxes.

The Bible also requires of us that we pray for all who are in authority, that we may lead "a quiet and peaceable life, in all godliness and honesty." What sort of a prayer would that man make who had just been cheating the Government out of taxes? And if a man prays for the Government, and prays honestly, and has any apprehension of the solemnity of addressing the Deity, he will not dare to cheat his Government if he has offered the prayer. And, perhaps, I ought to say that I fear here is a neglect on the part of the Church, that in our family prayers before our children we do not, as frequently as we ought, pray for our rulers; and that in leading the devotions of the house of God we are not as careful on this point as perhaps we ought to be. It is one of those practices that has its effect upon unpraying and irreligious men who are with us on such occasions. The good citizen prays for his rulers. It seems to me that Jesus Christ has settled this whole question. You will recollect that at one time the Pharisees sent to him certain persons to entrap him on political questions. There were political parties in his day, and they desired to commit him to one party or the other; and they sent persons to him for this purpose, to entangle him. After having complimented and flattered him by saying, "Master, we know that thou art true, and teachest the way of God in truth, neither carest thou for any man: for thou regardest not the person of men:" they ask him this question, "Tell us therefore, what thinkest thou? Is it lawful to give tribute unto Cesar, or not?"

Jesus said, "Show me the tribute money. And they brought unto him a penny. And he saith unto them, Whose is this image and superscription? They say unto him, Cesar's." It is one of the highest functions, if not the highest, of any Government to coin money, to fix the standard of values; and the Saviour understood that the individual whose image and superscription was on the money, was the supreme authority; and when they said unto him, "Cesar's," he said, "Render therefore unto Cesar the things which are Cesar's; and unto God the things that are God's." Meet your whole duty as citizens, and meet your obligations as Christians. They could not tell whether he was for Cesar or against Cesar, or, to modernize it, whether he was a Democrat or a Republican; and yet he settled that whole question of political obligations.

I hope I have made the distinctions plain—that we are to preach "as the oracles of God;" that we are to conform strictly to this rule, and only preach such subjects as we are taught by the Holy Scriptures. And I submit, brethren, who of us can desire to preach any thing else? Is there salvation in any other name but the name of Jesus? Is there any awakening, transforming, and sanctifying power in any truths but the truth of God? Will philosophy and astronomy convert the souls of men? Are we not sent for this purpose, to save men? and can we hope to fulfill that purpose in any other way than by preaching the gospel of the grace of God? "If any man speak, let him speak as the oracles of God." Have any of you preached all there is in the Bible, so that you must go somewhere else for truth? Have you given to the people all the unsearchable riches of Christ, so that you must go somewhere else for some other aliment with which to feed the flock of Christ? Is there no more variety in these spiritual topics, in these saving doctrines, in these sublime motives, in these precious promises, in these blessed exhortations of the Holy Scriptures? O, if any man speak, let him speak, and always speak, "as the oracles of God!"

And we must not only say the same things, but say them in the same order. There is an order in the Holy Scriptures, a purpose in the Bible; and every part of Holy Scripture is intended to promote that interest. There is one object in this watch, [taking out the watch and showing it.] It is to indicate to us the passing of time; and every part of the watch, every spring, and wheel, and post, and pin, is intended to promote that one object—the correct keeping and indication of time. So in these Holy Scriptures there is the same oneness; and every part of the Bible is intended to effect that one object, the recovery and restoration of our race, through the atonement and mediation of our Lord Jesus Christ. The Scriptures are a revelation. They give to us our knowledge of God and our knowledge of ourselves. But for these Holy Scriptures we should not have known the origin of our race, and, perhaps, should have been so ignorant and degraded that we might claim the ancestry of the monkey; but, thank God! we know we have a parentage divine. The Scriptures also give us a narration of facts in the history of our race; not only of our creation, but of the fall, and the promise of the Saviour; and the reason for that promise is known because the fall is stated before the promise. We have an account of the deluge. The reason for that destruction of the human family is given in the fact that the whole race had become corrupt before God. We have the giving of the law on Sinai—otherwise we should not understand the advent of Christ or the object of his vicarious death and of his glorious resurrection; for "by the law is the knowledge of sin," and the "law is our schoolmaster to bring us to Christ," as the only Saviour from sin.

There is also an order in religious experience. The individual must be enlightened, and have a conviction of his guiltiness before he will repent. He must be sorry for his sins after a godly sort before he can believe in Christ. He must believe in Christ in order to his justification and the concomitant blessings of regeneration and adoption. He must be justified before he is sanctified. He must be sanctified before he is glorified. Thus there is an order in the Scriptures; and in order that we may speak according to "the oracles of God" we must have this order in our teaching. We must begin at the right end, and lead the people on from one step to another in their knowledge and in their experience. It is necessary that we preach the law before we preach the Gospel. There is as much law in the New Testament as in the Old, though not in precisely the same form; and it is unfortunate, we think, in these latter days, that there is less of law and its claims preached than formerly, and that men do not see and feel its condemnation as they ought. Yet we would not confine any one, not even in a single sermon, to the law, for

"Law and terror do but harden
All the while they work alone,"

and therefore seem rather to make against the sinner's restoration; but, accompanied

> "By a sense of blood-bought pardon
> Melt and break the heart of stone."

The Law and the Gospel is the order which we find in the Holy Scriptures. A pastor should so systematize his teaching that each sermon should suggest the text and subject for the next discourse. Allowing for special occasions and subjects appropriate to them, still the preacher during his pastorate should seek to give his people the whole system of Bible truth in all its relations and applications. This is necessary in order to thoroughly indoctrinate and spiritually educate the people.

Again, we should preach in a style corresponding with that of the Bible. Each writer in Holy Scripture maintains his individuality. His style is personal. There is as much identity in the style as there is in the character of the writer. I can conceive of no inspiration that is not verbal. God takes the thoughts and words of these individuals, and so arranges them as to make them say what he would have said; and he allows every person who wrote and spoke as he was moved by the Holy Ghost to maintain his personal style. In like manner should every minister be himself. If Dr. Chalmers had undertaken to preach like Wesley, or Wesley like Dr. Chalmers, it would have been like David and Goliath exchanging their weapons of war. If Dr. Olin had attempted to preach like Dr. Fisk, or Dr. Fisk like Dr. Olin, it would have spoiled both these great and good men in their ministry. Let every man be himself in his preaching.

Nevertheless, there are some general characteristics of the style of the Bible which should be observed. One is directness. When we read the Bible we know who is meant, and we know what is meant. Its teaching is direct; it reaches the person, the character, the conscience, and the judgment for which it was intended. The style is beautiful, poetic, grandly figurative, and sometimes wonderfully logical; nevertheless, so simple that the wayfaring man, though a fool, need not err in reading it. So simple, so direct, is the style of Holy Scripture, that even he that runs may read.

Again, the style of the Bible is earnest and vehement. There is no indifference or carelessness in what the writer says; the very manner impresses the reader. We should also preach in the same spirit. What is the spirit of the Bible? The one pervading, all-animating, all-inspiring spirit is love. O, how God reveals his heart to us in those Holy Scriptures! Hear him saying, "How shall I give thee up!" "I have no pleasure in the death of him that dieth: . . . wherefore turn yourselves, and live ye." "Ho, every one that thirsteth, come ye to the waters, and he that hath no money; come ye, buy and eat." After he has once awakened a sinner, once arrested his attention, once softened his heart, and he resists and goes on in impenitence, he does not say, "Well, now, it is his fault: I have awakened him, I have interested him, I have given him the opportunity; and if he perish it is his own fault; I withdraw from him." O no; but he shows how great is his patience! how wonderful his forbearance! how continuous his strivings! Nothing but infinite love could manifest such persevering interest and such repeated efforts as God makes for the salvation of men! In order that we may fulfill our ministry we want a similar love—love that never fails, that endures all things, that never wearies; compassion that never is exhausted, and pity that never gives out. I would like to submit one thought more on this point.

We are to speak with corresponding authority. The apostle says, "Knowing therefore the terror of the Lord, we persuade men; but we are made manifest unto God, and I trust also are made manifest in your consciences." If the minister shows in his life that deadness to the world and that interest in his office which the apostle showed—if in his preaching his manner convinces the people that he believes what he says, that his heart is in it, that he is acting from convictions of duty, that he verily believes in God, in Jesus Christ, and in eternity—it will be made manifest in the consciences of his hearers; they will feel that he is an accredited embassador of Christ.

Furthermore, if all the doctrines which he states, if the truths which he presents, are not only sustained by argument but are also sanctioned by Scripture quotations—if there be a "thus saith the Lord" in it—he puts forth his statement and presentation of truth with the authority which is from heaven: not from himself, but from God, through his most holy word. He then becomes the mouth of God to the people, and the people so understand it. But above all, if his preaching is not in word only, but in demonstration of the Spirit and of power—if the unction of the Holy Ghost is upon him—if the divine

Spirit accompanies the word—then he speaks for God, he speaks as God, and God invests him with this authority. God demonstrates that authority by the accompanying power and influence of the Holy Spirit. When ministers have such a power accompanying their preaching, how mighty is the word of God to pull down the strongholds of Satan, and to save sinners! It is sharper than a two-edged sword.

"If any man minister, let him do it as of the ability which God giveth." I understand by this, pastoral work, so far as ministers are concerned; and I understand by pastoral work, pastoral ministrations, visiting the sick, relieving the poor, hunting up the lost, going after the straying, instructing the ignorant, sympathizing with the afflicted and despondent; comforting those who are in distress in estate, body, or mind; answering questions of casuistry; explaining to the people their temptations, and showing them how to escape from the snare of Satan; encouraging those who are halting, strengthening those who are weak, guiding those who are hesitating and erring; in short, in every possible way ministering to the bodily and spiritual necessities of the people; to their temporal as well as their eternal interests. The pastor's heart is a reservoir into which every spring of sorrow that breaks out in his congregation naturally flows. In doing this work, so complex, so responsible, and so urgent, the text says we must do it "as of the ability which God giveth."

I understand one element of this ability to be time, opportunity. In order that we may have this time, it is well for us to remember the first rule for a preacher in our Discipline: "Never be unemployed; never be triflingly employed ; never trifle away time ; neither spend any more time in any place than is strictly necessary."

The observance of that rule, and the systematizing of our action, will give to us enlarged opportunities for all this service. And, brethren, how precious is time for such a purpose ; how invaluable is time for such a use and end ! We "labor together with God" in the recovery and salvation of those who share our immortality and our capacities for bliss or woe. O, how dear to us should be every day, and every hour, and every part of time given to us, for the fulfilling of our holy ministry !

It does seem to me, that an hour of ministerial service on earth is worth more than an age of beatitude in eternity. I do feel that the opportunity to promote the eternal destiny of one spirit is worth more than the felicitating ourselves a whole cycle of eternity in heaven. There will be an eternity after that cycle is gone! but O, when time is gone the opportunity is lost! the occasion passes away, and can never be recalled ! the opportunity of taking one with us up to enjoy that eternity is forever beyond our reach ! Let Cleopatras dissolve and drink diamonds if they will ; let prodigals squander their inheritances if they will ; let kings give away crowns if they will ; let the worldlings kill time if they will ; but let the Christian minister use every inch and every moment of it in fulfilling the great mission to which his God has called him.

Another element of this ability is health. Our labors must and will be proportioned, more or less, to our physical strength. That is an unavoidable necessity. Consequently, health to a minister is most precious. He cannot, therefore, without sin, knowingly do any thing, or indulge in any habit or practice, that impairs his physical vigor; he must, therefore, avoid all excesses—whether in eating, drinking, or sleeping. On the other hand, he is under obligation to do every thing that he knows will promote his health and strength. I believe most conscientiously—and I have no wavering in my convictions on that subject—that there are many occasions in the life of a Christian minister when it is his duty not only to risk health, but even life, to carry out the work which God has intrusted to him; and our world will not be saved without the sacrifice of many human lives. And when that belief comes upon a man he cannot shirk it. He is under higher obligation to submit to that danger, and to that death, if it come, than is the soldier in the service of the State. Nevertheless, before he does that he should be certain of the requirement—that the exigency exists, that the interest involved makes it a duty. Up to that point he is bound by his obligations to God and the Church, in the execution of his high commission, to take the utmost care of his health, and to preserve his strength, that he may have them for the furtherance of this work and the accomplishment of this ministry.

General information is another element. A man may be learned in the sciences, he may be what we call a polished scholar, and yet he may have so little knowledge of men and things as to be but poorly qualified to be an adviser to his people in their duties, to be a comforter to them in their trials, to be a help to them in the difficulties in which they are involved. In order that he may be able to advise safely, prudently, and wisely in all these questions that appropriately come before him from his people, he must be, as we have said, a man of general information, and a careful, critical observer of men and things ; a man of experience, thought, reflection, and study, examining and analyzing all those interests to which his attention may be called, and where his counsel may be needed. He must be deeply versed in spiritual things in order that he may instruct his people in all those questions of religious experience submitted to him ; in all those subtle devices of Satan, in all those various temptations, in all the influences which affect religious experience. How extensive and accurate should be his knowledge of all these subjects, in order that he may be prepared for this office and work!

Another element is sympathy. Some men, good men, repel persons by the rigidness of their manners and austerity of their appearance. They do not intend to do it, but that has become their habit, and by that severity of demeanor they keep their people at a distance from them ; and though they would go to their pastor for counsel and comfort, many of them have not the confidence to do so. It is, therefore, necessary that the pastor shows sympathy with his people in all their interests and in all their welfare. They must believe that he loves them, that he will have the patience and the kindness to hear them, that he will have the sympathy that will lead him to do as much as in him lies to help them, and that they will have his counsel, his agency, and his prayers for their deliverance out of all their troubles. This sympathy is essential to us in meeting those obligations that come upon us in our pastoral relations to the people committed to our charge.

And all these things are to be done, the text says, "Of the ability which God giveth." Certainly, God gives us our time and our health; but he gives us all these blessings, all this ability, on the same condition upon which he gives us other blessings. He gives the husbandman his harvest, but the husbandman must sow or else he cannot reap. He gives to us the fruits of our industry, but we must labor before we receive them. He gives us knowledge, but we must seek it before we possess it. He gives us salvation, but we must pray for it before we enjoy it. So with this ability. We must seek it and pray for it. We must watch as well as pray and labor for it, in order that we may enjoy it; and if we, as we have already intimated, husband our time, systematize the manner in which we employ it, our days will be lengthened thereby so far as results are concerned, and opportunities given for greater usefulness. Our health is also a subject for which we may legitimately pray; it is included in our prayer for our daily bread. And this knowledge of which we have spoken must be sought; we must study and labor for it; and this tenderness of heart, this gentleness of spirit, this kindness of manner, this sweetness of temper, is the gift of the Holy Spirit, and God can invest every one of us with it in all its fullness, so that we may every one have the spirit that was in our Lord Jesus Christ.

Let us now look at the motive presented: "That God in all things may be glorified through Jesus

Christ." It is a wonderful question to submit to a human being—how he can glorify the Infinite; and yet, evidently, the fact is set forth here, that it is our prerogative to glorify God through Jesus Christ. God is glorified when he is revealed to intelligent beings; when his attributes are made known to those who can in some measure understand and appreciate them. No intelligent and holy being can have a just conception of God without being filled with adoration, without being constrained to homage and to worship; and when God is revealed to men he not only excites their adoration and praise, but he calls out their trust, confidence, and love, so that the revelation of God to the human family contributes to his honor, and advances his declarative glory in the earth. God is glorified when any of his plans and purposes are consummated, for he certainly makes no plan and engages in no enterprise which is not worthy of him. And this certainly is true of the great plan of salvation by which lost men are recovered from sin, and restored to his nature, image, and fellowship. When this scheme of redemption and mercy, for the accomplishment of which he gave his only and well-beloved Son to die, is advanced, promoted, and extended in the earth—when its consummation is hastened, when its purposes are being fulfilled—certainly God is glorified. His praise and glory are extended, and his name and character exalted among the subjects over whom he reigns. Consequently, whenever an individual is converted; when a human heart is filled with holy love; when another soul is brought into the fruition of God; when other lips are employed in the praise of God; when another trophy of the cross is redeemed and brought into salvation, into a safe relation to the spirit-world; when the great choir of heaven and earth, who are united in his praise, is multiplied; when the tide of this praise rises higher and higher before his throne—God is glorified. And when, through our pastoral care as well as our pulpit services, Christians are edified, and built up, and sustained in their warfare; when they are led on to the highest experiences, and the holiest lives, and the happiest deaths; when they are brought into the presence and society of the spirits of the just made perfect; when they are planted before the throne; when God sees in them his image and "the purchase of his blood;" when he sees in them the recovery of his lost ones, and the restoration of his sinful ones—when he thus sees in and through eternity these results of the scheme of redemption and mercy, surely his glory is promoted. His glory is advanced every time, then, that there is a penitent sigh awakened and a penitent prayed offered.

Every time that a soul testifies to salvation; every time that there is a new joy among the angels in heaven; every time that another spirit is translated from earth to heaven; every time that a new note is added to the praise of the spirit-world—God, through our humble ministration, is exalted, is magnified, is glorified. O what a motive is this! what sublimity it gives to life! what interest it gives to every religious effort! what grandeur it gives to our administrations! what felicity it gives to our hearts! what joy comes back upon our souls! If one of us knew today that by traveling a hundred miles on foot we could find Charlie Ross and restore him to his parents, we would start, without going home to say "Good-bye" to our families, and we would persist in it through weariness and difficulty until we had carried him and given him to the embrace of his sorrowing parents; and when we had done that, O what a satisfaction, what a grateful and triumphant joy, would fill our hearts! How sweetly we should sleep, how happily we should live, after we had accomplished that result!

Now, here are around us thousands of children that are lost to their heavenly Parent; they are away from home; they are on the dark mountains of sin. Perhaps they are in the very dens of iniquity around us, and they may be very near the gates of hell! And yet they are in time; they are in probation; and we, the embassadors, the representatives, of Jesus Christ, are sent to "seek and to save them that are lost." If we gather one of these precious souls and bring it back to the bosom of God, and in the day of judgment may say to Jesus Christ, "Here am I, and a trophy of my ministry," what felicity will be ours! what reward will come to our souls! what recompense to us for our fidelity and success in our holy pastorate, in our Christian ministry!

The Bible begins with a statement of fact; it ends with a benediction: "The grace of our Lord Jesus Christ be with you all. Amen."

www.ingramcontent.com/pod-product-compliance
Lightning Source LLC
LaVergne TN
LVHW011133110826
845150LV00008B/2328
* 9 7 8 1 4 1 8 1 9 5 0 1 4 *